Invisible
Sun

Invisible
Sun

Richard Skinner

Smokestack Books
1 Lake Terrace, Grewelthorpe,
Ripon HG4 3BU
e-mail: info@smokestack-books.co.uk
www.smokestack-books.co.uk

ISBN 9781838198817

Smokestack Books
is represented
by Inpress Ltd

Acknowledgements

Thanks are due to the editors of the following print and online publications in which all these poems first appeared: *Anthropocene, Coast to Coast to Coast, Fenland Poetry Journal, Finished Creatures, The High Window, Mediterranean Poetry, One Hand Clapping, Pamenar, Reliquiae, Seek, Strands, Writers' Cafe.*

'Topoi of Epic' was first published in the anthology *Millets* (Zeno Press, 2017), with thanks to Christian Patracchini.

'Winterborne' was first published in *Winter Solstice Anthology* (Writers' Cafe Magazine, 2018), with thanks to Marie Lightman.

'Boxes' was first published in *Eighty Four: Poems on Male Suicide, Vulnerability, Grief and Hope* (Verve Poetry Press, 2019), with thanks to Helen Calcutt.

'Organ of Corti' was shortlisted for the 2019 Well Review prize and was set to music and released on *Salt of the Earth Vol.2* (2021), with thanks to Will Lawton.

'*Trans limen ad lumen*' was first published in the *Earth Shadow Anthology* (Poetry Village, 2020), with thanks to David Coldwell.

'Their Heads Are Green and Their Hands Are Blue' was first published in *Writing Utopia* (Hesterglock Press, 2020), with thanks to Sarer Scotthorne & Sally-Shakti Willow.

Thanks for comments and support Jill Abram, Mona Arshi, Jean Atkin, Clodagh Beresford Dunne, Stephanie Bowgett, Iris Colomb, Joey Connolly, Anthony Costello, Jacqueline Crooks, Patrick Davidson Roberts, Nichola Deane, Josephine Dickinson, Andrea Gibellini, David Harsent, Lisa Kelly, Victoria Kennefick, Evalyn Lee, Martin Malone, Dan O'Brien, Lani O'Hanlon, Autumn Richardson, Anna Saunders, Richard Scott, Kelley K. Swain.

Special thanks to Roy Marshall for his help with formatting and sequencing.

*'C'est l'envers qui
vous dit la vérité.'*
Louise
Bourgeois

Contents

Trans limen ad lumen

Sudden sun on stone in drenched Richmond –
a burning bridge. The disintegration has begun.
The low sun on the river is a white flame.
Select your steps with care and move toward the light.

The High Street Inversions

i

On the wet lowlands,
            we are in a fret & haar
        of hazy whiteness,
wheeling us amnesiac.

ii

The corried slopes
                draw us up
                        into cloud,
                                then fade...

iii

            As we climb,
        the mind
                empties in in-
        crements.

iv

Clear of the scar, we meet the spirit-
                level
where cloud & air collide.

v

In a blink, there
is a rinse
of blue. Below,
cloud fills
valley; above,
each crag & gully
is   translucent.

vi

The now upside-
        down world
               is a cloud-
      less sky, a blue
  liquidity.
      Or is it sea?

vii

    The air thins
    & clarifies me
    to an
    apex of
    being.

viii

In a squint,
the sun is a sparkler,
& all the west is shining.

Corridors & Wards

I   The Island of Doubt

What are these? Toothpicks or cocktail sticks? They are so fiddly.
Why are they so difficult to pick up? What are those sounds on
the roof? Birds? Are we near the sea? Who is that in the
photograph? No, it's not me. I never had my hair like that. Why
are your feet blue? Oh, they're shoes? I have no feeling in my
feet. If I fall, how will you pick me up? Oh, it's pathetic, isn't it?
Will someone please answer that phone? Is this medicine? How
is your mother? How did she look? *Like you do right now.* No,
I'm not tired. I lay awake all night. Can I get there by candlelight?
Yes, and back again. Oh I have been to Ludlow fair and left my
necklace God knows where. Are there still cedars in Lebanon?
Are there gales in Lundy? Are they drowning the meadows? Am
I standing in a stream? I can hear water. I am water gifted. I
remember the dropped glass in the stream. The silence was full
of birds. Wherever I am, I am what's missing. Whatever's
missing is where love has gone. Which of these voices is mine?
Few. But roses.

II   The Egg

I am holding an egg
in my hand.
One of life's joys.
So perfect in shape.
So simple, yet complex.

But, of course,
I'm not really talking
about an egg.
I'm really talking
about my mother.

The egg is just a portal,
a vehicle merely to talk
about my mother.
Not one of life's joys.
Not simple, but still complex.

What's a poem for?
To unlock the secrets
of the universe.
To release the potential
of inanimate objects,

like eggs and mothers,
which are both part
of the same big question,
which I can and can't talk about
in a poem.

III   Rooms

I am moving through the rooms.
Someone has turned me inside out and now
all my bad decisions are on show.
This juice is good but the beaker is too big.
This machine looks just like the sun.
1... 2... 3... 4...
My arms are electronic.
Twice I fought with the devil last night.
There is ash on my forehead.
The view from this room is nice –
a garden of reflection. Hills.

IV   My mother's things

i.m. Diana Malcolm Cartland, née Greig, 1941–2019

Four Dior Addict 754 lipsticks
(Vibrant colour! Spectacular shine!).
Rolex Depose # Yoke/Sc x1.
A tape measure, pins & needles.
Three Radley purses (empty).
Photos in sepia of her Grandfather 'Jimmy' Leggat
(a ne'er-do-well from Airdrie),
her mother Jan on her wedding day
& her father Alec in Captain's uniform in Cairo.
A yellow yo-yo.

Azahar

Mid-air, head-over-heels, a peeled hare
in a sack of yoke is hauled
through oil. The two buds inside it tap
and bulge and then, at the slack tide
of 26 weeks, the Cremaster forces them
to sink or swim, turning them into peaches
or pearls.

On a slope in Andalucia, rows of orange trees
squirt their scent, giving birth to a word: *azahar*.
Below ground, a chimera fuses
with the rootstock,
a new citrus effervesces, suckers sprout
and a different fruit yolks to the stem – the oranges
cede to the usurper lemon.

Candling

Mrs Miller lies prone and stoned,
gazing at a marble egg,
tracing the red lines of rivers on fire,
the dull glare of invisible suns.

The Winter Lady's head
as graceful as a Grecian urn,
the blue veins snaking through,
mottling the alien skin.

Checking the egg for flaws
she holds it up to the candle, then
checking her heart for the missing beat,
she finds a bullet in the bible.

Topoi of Epic

Over there is the distant glitter of other peoples' lives.
Light that comes, light that goes.
Faces against the glass whisper their preferred seasons.
Let us remain open to small inheritances.

Light that comes, light that goes.
A simple way to go faster than light that does not work.
Let us remain open to small inheritances.
A planet, a *sol niger* (boredom), drifts into view.

A simple way to go faster than light that does not work.
Stillness is not achieved by stopping but by meeting yourself, head-on.
A planet, a *sol niger* (boredom), drifts into view.
All the trees north of you are clear, all the birds have flown south.

Stillness is not achieved by stopping but by meeting yourself, head-on.
Faces against the glass whisper their preferred seasons.
All the trees north of you are clear, all the birds have flown south.
Over there is the distant glitter of other peoples' lives.

Organ of Corti

In order to reach the centre, we must turn away
because we are bound by walls, we cannot go where we like.
Our mind is shaped as a maze is wrought –
the life of the mind, the knot in the beard.

We are bound by walls, we cannot go where we like.
The figure in the carpet, hidden in plain sight,
the life of the mind, the knot in the beard.
The still intense sun of a late afternoon.

The figure in the carpet, hidden in plain sight.
Each time we make a choice, we lose a little more
of the still intense sun of a late afternoon.
We follow the path offered in order to reach the centre

and each time we make a choice, we lose a little more
of our mind that is shaped as a maze is wrought.
We follow the path offered in order to reach the centre
and in order to reach the centre, we must turn away.

White Balloons

after Sampaolo's 'Fantasticherie Infantili'

The first nurse, Ida Sessions, carries her white balloon –
it is heavy as lead, dead weight.
She lives with it, calls it her monkey.

The second nurse, Jackie Lemancyzk, is a carer, a
dreamer. Her white balloon
is going to carry her away, one day.

The third nurse, ID Unknown, is more earnest.
She tussles with her white balloon,
legs akimbo, telling it off
for aimless wandering.

The land is scrub, the trees low and gnarled,
their few leaves a blur.
The *casa blanca* on the horizon
hasn't been lived in for years.

Boxes

You always hated my boxes.
The black belt box with its gold lettering;
the Art Nouveau tin of mints from Montreaux;
the red marbled box that held a bottle of wine.

You never understood why I
kept them in my wardrobe. The top cupboard
in the kitchen is always empty. 'Why?' you asked.

Then your mother died and you snapped like elastic.
Your breath turned sour and you drank wine
all of the day and all of the night.

Our grief composes itself in the whole space
of the upper body and comparts itself
into packets, boxes
that only then can I throw away.

The Strata Building

Every window in the block
has a hooded figure in it,
maybe an anorak on a hanger,
or a jacket on a hatstand.
Or just people standing,
staring out over the city at night.
It's difficult to tell
from this distance.

Millions of people come through here.
People of every colour,
all hooded, voiceless.
They made it from some distant shore,
up the beach, over
a bridge and onto a road,
where they start to walk.
They start to walk faster and faster,
then they are running.
I've heard that people run all the time
in the north country.

But the people here
are not at war.
They only stand and stare
out the windows of their block.
Perhaps they are ghosts.
The hungry ghosts
of all those who didn't make it
and never will.

I want to reach out and touch them,
to lay my hands on their chest,
to energise their heart.
I cannot give them anything they need.
I cannot give them more life,
just leprosy.
Their hoods might turn into cowls
for the dead, which we remove
before placing in trucks,
which drive all night
to the north country.

I want to reach out and touch them,
to lay my hands on their chest,
to energise their heart, turn
the distance they have covered
into something more
than standing at a window
staring out over the city at night.
I want to see the truth in their hearts,
which I know will be there.
I want to see the whites of their eyes
before I make a promise.

Their Heads are Green
and their Hands are Blue

So, it is time to leave. Stay in groups,
pairs at least,
do not wander off alone.
If you must go your own way, make sure you have a horn
and a net. Do not worry about the noises
coming from the bushes to the side.
Keep your eyes ahead, one drop of fear
and they will strike. Steer by the stars but,
remember, when the water flows the other way,
the stars have turned upside down.
You are lucky if you see the goldsmoke.
You will have sage on your hands, to heal,
and wind at your feet, to fly.
When they speak a language you do not know,
you are safe,
but only for a few days. Do not stay
for they will think you are real. Stand up,
make the sign,
be ready to go. The time is now;
in the distance lies the future.
There is so much space ahead of you,
so much dark land.

Zuihitsu

I   On painting a chrysanthemum

If you want to paint a chrysanthemum, look at one
for ten years until you become one.

II   The narrow road to the deep interior

The distance between
the rim of the tea cup
and your lip, I shall trace.
The way your head rests, Empress,
upon the pillow.

Later, through a window,
I will study
the distance between
branches of a bush,
involving the wind.

My mind is a running brush
between these spaces
(there is no central point),
building images as clouds drifting
with a volcano wrapped within.

III   In praise of shadows

The story of the Zen master
        who painted a landscape so perfect
                that he walked into it
                        and disappeared.

IV   The form of an object is a diagram of the forces acting upon it

Snowflakes are fractal records of the changing circumstances that ice encounters during its descent. No two falling snowflakes will meet the same circumstances; no two snowflakes will be identical.

V   The faraway place

I have a twin brother and,
when I was two years old,
one of us – the other one –
was kidnapped. He was taken
to a faraway place
and we haven't seen each other since.
I think my protagonist is him.
A part of myself, but not me.

VI   The tower of mirrors

A Zen buddhist monk is walking in the forest and watches a group of children at play. He sees beautiful red flowers and falls into a dream where he is in a tower full of thousands of mirrors, each with a name beneath it, and when he looks into a mirror, he enters that world. Places such as the world of the future, or of the ancients, or of oblivion. The monk has entered the green world of the tower, a place where the artificial is real and the real is deluded. The monk does not know that this tower is a dream world until he awakes to find that he has been trapped by a demon fish with blue eyes, called a Ch'ing, which has exposed his own mind to himself, his tangled web of consciousness, and the trappings of his desires and seductions, as nothing more than a dream.

VII   Gong!

let the sounds be louder

and louder yet   far into sleep

each is longer because   dripping into the forest

one waits to the very end   the sounds

of the resonances   the stroke that starts

the tone

Ariadne

I felt him coming to our seaborne empire
for me. I felt my love coming.
His desire was greater than the distance
that kept us apart.

My heart has always been plush
since my upbringing in the prerogatives.
My father, my King,
so wise, senescent and cunning too.

When the boat came, my heart stopped.
He was so handsome. Through the overcrowded gaze,
I could feel his heat on me.
My heart was speechless.

Then he entered the maze.
When I felt the red thread's tug,
I knew he was alive. Joy!
And when he emerged –

we fled.
Naxos is a dream.
That night, he fled me.
I feigned sleep.

Then, cymbals and timbales woke me, really.
And there he was, head of the procession.
The women wild, horses hooves and tails, goat heads.
'I am a god. What's the mystery?'

I closed my eyes the night I became his wife.
I held the globe in my head, red thread covering it like a
                                                    cobweb.
I hear him still. I hear him.
Life is wanting one thing but getting another.

Test to assess whether or not a person is suffering from amnesia

A man wearing a toga is standing on a platform that is just under the surface of the water about 50m off the coast of the Greek island of Andros. He is clutching a hard copy of a score of an opera by Thomas Adès. Another man is swimming towards him. The sea is rough.

a) Is the standing man a Virgo or a Capricorn?
b) Is the boat sailing towards them blue or green?
c) Why are the people on the beach running away?
d) Do you like yoga?
q) What is the difference between a dwarf and a child?
t) Is it a Tuesday or a Saturday?
j) Why is the man on the boat laughing? What is his name?
k) Are the standing man's eyes blue or green?
s) Where is the octopus?

The Number Poem

for Roy Marshall

Hands, aid, light and degrees are all first; hands and degrees can be second; only degrees can be third.

Timings and tones come in twos; the number of backs a beast has; the number of heads that are better.

Stooges and wise men; dimensions and a card trick; a number to be the best of, but not in a crowd.

Leafed clovers, the best of a kind at poker, the number of posts on a bed. Winds, Tops, fab.

High, take, gimme. Fingers, senses, the o'clock shadow, the sided star.

The number of feet under, and a half dozen of the other. Packs, nations, shooters. The worst companion for sevens.

The worst companion for sixes. The Ancient Wonders of the world. Dwarves, sisters, deadly sins, seas, yearly itches.

Hard, figure of, middle. Pieces of, folds.

The whole number of yards; the number of stitches saved; the number of lives a cat has.

Commandments.

The Grief Directory

I thought that having lost my father as a child I understood loss – but a mother is a very particular thing, which one knows in the living and brutally relearns in the loss. (Margot)

Losing one's mother is life changing. It doesn't matter how old or young your mother (or you are), it's your mother. The rest of your life will be shaped by it. But it will be ok. (Helen Y)

Yes, grief is a tricky one and takes its own time to work through. Keep talking about the feelings, however difficult it might seem. It does help. Mind how you go. (Paul H)

We only have one mother. The roots and tendrils of that relationship beginning long before memory. Death is always tough. All the best for the road ahead. Good luck. (Sam)

Grief takes its own goddamned time. And it's kinda empty words to point that out, but it will subside. All about (and isn't it a silly term) self-care at this stage. I find swimming helps. (Ben)

Grief thing is entirely specific to the person – let it be about you. (Pat)

You're vulnerable and in shock. Anger is based on safety. Go with it. (Kay)

Loss is hard, it takes tolls in all kinds of ways, both expected and unexpected. (Laura C)

Sky with Four Suns

after John Luther Adams

The first sun – a time bomb – was sucked
into a black bucket and then –
boom. Its igneous
nodes touched and sparked a blackout
for aeons.

The second sun was ferrous,
burnished as a shield,
only coming into focus
when it burned redly through
the blizzards.

The third sun was a blank
placeholder, a luminous ring
empty inside –
a winter-white afterglow
rather than a furnace.

The fourth sun – our sun –
is a yellow light of feeling in
our plastic Holocene. We kick it
with our kharmic footprints
but it is still to yield,
yet even light has a shelf life.

Mists

We must learn to love the mists,
the way they waft through us,
making the day larger
more autumnal,
turning our skins translucent
to soften our silhouette
so that we no longer
block out bits of the sun.

Winterborne

Winter Solstice, 2017

Across the river and into the trees,
the frightened trees,
I am a man lost in space
hurtling through a green passage.
Every false morning is a wonder.
I am here in the world with you,
this white-on-white world,
to see you safely into the day,
to say that you are dead; now live your life.